Perspectives from a "SMART" Christian

Finding JOY in Life's Difficulties

Perspectives from a "SMART" Christian

Karla Christian

WORD AFLAME PRESS

Perspectives from a "Smart" Christian

by Karla Christian

Cover design and photography by Ben Meydam

Pictured on cover, Kara Christian

Copyright © 2007, Word Aflame Press

All Scripture quotations in this book are from the King James Version of the Bible unless otherwise identified.

All rights reserved. No portion of this publication may be reproduced, stored in an electronic system, or transmitted in any form or by any means, electronic, mechanical, photocopy, recording, or otherwise, without the prior permission of Word Aflame Press. Brief quotations may be used in literary reviews.

Printed in United States of America

WORD AFLAME PRESS
8855 Dunn Road, Hazelwood, MO 63042
www.pentecostalpublishing.com

Library of Congress Cataloging-in-Publication Data

Christian, Karla, 1957–
   Perspectives from a "Smart" Christian / by Karla Christian.
      p. cm.
   ISBN 978-1-56722-708-6
1. Happiness—Religious aspects—Christianity. 2. Christian life. I. Title.
BV4647.J68C5 2007
248.4—dc22

                                                                  200610147

Dedication

To my wonderful and vibrant daughters,
Kara, Courtney, and Kalee,
who have brought joy beyond measure
into my life. I love you dearly.

Contents

Introduction 9

Acknowledgments 13

INTERVAL 1:
   The Good Outweighs the Bad 17

INTERVAL 2:
   Our Pursuit of Happiness 21

INTERVAL 3:
   Father Knows Best 25

INTERVAL 4:
   Smile Awhile. 29

INTERVAL 5:
   No Fear 33

INTERVAL 6:
   Still Crazy after All These Years 39

INTERVAL 7:
   The Joy of Children 45

INTERVAL 8:
   Too Much to Do. 51

INTERVAL 9:
   Touching the Lives of Others 55

INTERVAL 10:
   One of Those Bad Days. 59

INTERVAL 11:
    Don't Let the Grouches Get You Down 65
INTERVAL 12:
    The Best Response. 69
INTERVAL 13:
    Finding Gladness. 75
INTERVAL 14:
    Share the Joy. 79
INTERVAL 15:
    The Power of Words 83
INTERVAL 16:
    Only God Can Change Lives,
    but We Can Help! 87
INTERVAL 17:
    Celebrating Friendships 93
INTERVAL 18:
    Tough Times. 99
INTERVAL 19:
    And How Do You Like Your Job?. 105
INTERVAL 20:
    How Do You Affect Your Atmosphere? 111
INTERVAL 21:
    Ending on a Happy Note. 115

Introduction

It is a sunny, fall day, and here I sit unable to be out enjoying the wonderful, brisk weather. Poor me! My throbbing foot reminds me again of the recent surgery and the doctor's explicit instructions about "staying off" the foot if I want to avoid severe consequences. Well, what are my options? I can sit here feeling sorry for myself, or I can think of my blessings and count them one by one.

Face it! Along with the good that comes our way, we will deal with adversities and trials. I marvel at some people who face so many obstacles yet have the positive attitude and belief that things will be all right. I also see that for others the slightest bump in the road throws their lives into a state of chaos.

How we handle our struggles will determine what kind of people we really are. What kind of person am I? I have asked myself that question many times and have decided it is not an easy one to answer. However, there are a few characteristics I would like to develop. I want to be a person whom people look to when they need uplifting. I would love to be able to bring a bit of cheer into someone's seemingly hopeless situation. I want to be an encourager to those around me. I want to look for

◦ Perspectives from a "Smart" Christian

the good in life instead of seeing only the bad, which is not easy in today's world.

Since I am "laid up," it is not easy to find something to occupy my time. I have listened to the radio a great deal; however, I have found that perhaps this is not the best encouragement for one in my circumstances. For instance, I am already feeling sorry for myself, and these are the reports I hear: "Gas prices are soaring. Heating oil and natural gas prices will double during the coming winter." Isn't that encouraging? Oh, wait! I think I hear some good news: "Elections are being held in Iraq. For the first time, many people will have the opportunity to vote on a constitution." I'm thinking, "That is so neat! I know they are excited." But then the report continues. "U.S. troops and Iraqi police are expecting attacks and bombings everywhere to try to stop the elections." Oh, well! A brief flicker of hope; then it is quashed again.

Perhaps the newspaper will offer more encouragement than the radio, I think as I reach for the daily edition. Unfortunately, the headlines are far from encouraging. The front-page headlines read, "Trash hauler seeks fuel surcharge," or "Councilman files suit against 3 newspapers," or "Former Illinois governor convicted of racketeering, fraud." Now, where I am from, this is really devastating: "Cardinals take a fall in the playoffs." I once heard a song that said, "Sure could use a little good news today," and I

Introduction

believe I am at that point. I realize we need to be adults and face the brutality of reality. However, why are we constantly bombarded with the bad news instead of the good? What can we do to help change the negative mind-set that fills our world?

Now, the Lord did not appear to me in a vision or a dream, neither did He speak to me in an audible voice. But I do believe I have received a little insight. We as children of God can help with all this negativity that bombards us on a daily basis by *looking for the good*. Isn't that profound? I know you were impacted with this deep enlightenment. I sincerely believe that if we look for the good in life's situations, peace and joy will become dominant in our lives—the peace, joy, and happiness that God desires for us to experience in our walk with Him.

If you take the time to read this *bookella* (not quite a book, but not a booklet), I trust you will take on the challenge of looking for the good or the positive side of life and will see how much brighter and sunnier things can be. If you do not have the time to read the entire volume in one sitting, take time for an "interval" or two whenever time allows.

Acknowledgments

First and foremost, thanks to my all-powerful Savior and Friend, Jesus Christ, who has changed the impossible to the possible time and time again.

To my parents, Jim Bob and Wanda Smart, thank you for the wonderful growing-up years. Most of all, thank you for instilling in me the desire to serve God and showing me how much fun it can be.

To our friends for life, Jerry and Phyllis Jones, thanks for your constant encouragement and incredible friendship. Your contribution to our lives is far more than could ever be expressed in words.

To all of my family, I thank God for you and am so thankful that you really are "my family"—my sister, Vicki; Joe; Geoff; Shanna; Aunt Doris and the rest of the Hapke crew; and especially Alex, our little joy seeker.

To some of our awesome friends, the Rick Flowers family, the Darrell Johns family, and the Terry Pugh family, thank you for providing support and wonderful times of fun and fellowship through the years. Thanks for being there for us.

To Reverend and Mrs. J. T. Pugh, who played such an integral role in our lives, thank you. You were the ideal example to us in our start as a young ministry team. Your

∽ Perspectives from a "Smart" Christian

patient mentoring, encouragement, and kindness to us will always be remembered.

To Robert Fuller, editor in chief, thank you for your advice throughout this whole process, and thanks for the chance to have fun as well by exchanging wit and witticisms. To Margie McNall, thank you for your guidance and professional help through this, my first endeavor in publication. To Ben Meydam, thank you for a tremendous job on your graphic design of the cover. And thanks to everyone who had a hand in completing this project. Forgive me if I failed to mention your name, for I sincerely appreciate your efforts.

To the remarkable crew of Church Administration, with whom I work on a daily basis (especially Diana Dunlap, Susan Fuller, Diana Jolley, and the one and only Brad Parker), thank you for so kindly tolerating my "I'm an authoress" syndrome and for making the workplace so enjoyable.

Thanks to the people who shared with me their various stories, thus contributing to the thoughts and materials in each Interval (chapter).

Special thanks go to Mary Wallace, who initiated the publishing of my first writings and editorials and never failed to tell me that I had a talent for writing.

Special thanks to my friend, Barbara Westberg, who became my encourager and a tremendous source of advice about writing when I first began.

And I give special thanks to First Lady Joy Haney for reaching into my heart with skilled hands and opening a

Acknowledgments

renewed window of hope about writing. The blessing of her confidence has given me additional courage to write and share the experiences of my life related in this book.

Last, but certainly not least, to my incredible, patient husband who should be awarded a medal of honor for living in "the girls' dorm." Thanks for keeping me calm and steady through both the good and bad times. I love you more than words could express.

INTERVAL 1

The Good Outweighs the Bad

Since I am incapacitated, my girls enjoy ministering to me. I have no choice but to sit and listen to their stories and help with their homework. I can't get up and walk away. They have Mom right where they want me. One afternoon Courtney decided to read me the copy of the Declaration of Independence that my husband had brought back from a recent trip to Washington, DC. (Now you know how bored I was!) I was merely tolerating her recitation when she read, "We hold these truths to be self-evident: That all men are created equal; that they are endowed by their Creator with certain unalienable rights; that among these are life, liberty, and the pursuit of happiness." I stopped Courtney and asked her to read that statement again. Our country's forefathers included in the Declaration of Independence this statement, that our Creator wanted us to have life, liberty, and the pursuit of happiness. I am humbled when I think of the struggles they endured and the sacrifices they made, leaving their homes, their wealth, and their families because the English government had suppressed their rights to life, liberty, and the pursuit of happiness.

Happiness could be defined as experiencing the sheer joy of being alive. We all want happiness, but to obtain it, one needs to pursue it. Happiness doesn't just happen.

I had a wonderful father-in-law who did not earn prestigious academic degrees, but he had a marvelous grasp of life. If my husband or his brothers ever felt down or blue, he would say, "Come on, boys, make yourselves happy." In other words, they could feel down and despondent if they wanted, but they were the only ones who could change how they felt. We can be "down in the doldrums" if we want, but we can find something to be happy about if we just look around.

"Down in the doldrums" was a cliché my parents used to describe my location when I was feeling blue. I had never really thought about what the doldrums meant until my youngest daughter, Kalee, asked me to help her study for a science test. One of the questions asked, "What is the windless part of the earth around the equator called?" The answer was, "the doldrums." Kalee explained that the doldrums are located in the middle of the ocean and that sailors avoid them. I had an epiphany from an elementary science lesson! If we are in the doldrums, we are in the middle of nowhere; nothing is happening and no one wants to join us. We certainly do not want to get caught in the doldrums, because it is difficult to sail through life when we are trapped in a motionless existence.

While flipping through a magazine, I noticed a page entitled "Words to Live By." At the bottom of the page a statement read, "Think of all the beauty still left around you, and be happy." I thought, *What a wonderful statement!* Then I glanced at the author's name and was quite surprised because the quote was attributed to Anne Frank. Many of us are familiar with the story of Anne Frank. She was a young Jewish girl who, with her family, spent two anxious years hiding from the German Nazis in a secret apartment above the shop where her father had worked. She kept a diary of her thoughts and the happenings in her narrow existence. I am awed by Anne's attitude. In spite of her dire circumstances, she still looked for the good in her life. She still found beauty around her and wanted others to be happy as well.

The Lord sometimes chooses interesting ways to get our attention, such as Anne Frank's simple statement, made while she was in the crosscurrents of dreariness and danger. Here I am, feeling somewhat out of sorts because of my pain and immobility, until Anne's words make me realize how fortunate and

Perspectives from a "Smart" Christian

blessed I am. I have three girls fetching and carrying anything I need, a husband dashing to the Quick Trip to get me a diet coke in a bottle because the aluminum can does not taste right, and a comfortable, cozy chair to sit in. How does this weigh out? The bad side: my foot hurts and I can't go anywhere. The good side: three girls who are serving as "go-fers," a wonderful husband who is, at this precise moment, sweeping the floor and straightening the house, a cold diet coke in a bottle, and a comfortable chair beside a cozy fire. When comparisons are made and all the facts are considered, the good far outweighs the bad.

INTERVAL 2

Our Pursuit of Happiness

What is happiness to you? Is it that beautiful dress you purchased for the upcoming Christmas banquet? Is it the smell of your brand-new car when you open the door? Or perhaps it is that bargain you got on that exquisite pair of shoes. Sometimes we pursue happiness in the wrong places. We think happiness is found in material possessions. We spend a great deal of energy on the "if onlys": If only I could get a new car, I would be happy. If only I could remodel my kitchen. If only I had leather living-room furniture instead of this battered and stained wood and chintz. And I'm so tired of raking this ratty, 1970s shag carpet! If only I had easy-care Berber. Unfortunately, when one "if only" is achieved, we add more "if onlys" to our list.

There was once a rich man who was near death. He had worked relentlessly for his money and could not bear to leave it behind. So he prayed

∞ Perspectives from a "Smart" Christian

that he would be allowed to take his wealth with him to heaven.

The Lord heard his plea and sent an angel to tell the rich man that it would do no good to liquidate his real estate holdings, sell his stock, or empty his bank accounts because he could not take it all with him. The man continued to whine and wheedle, and the Lord finally agreed to let him bring whatever he could stuff into one suitcase. The man rejoiced at his good fortune, found his largest suitcase, and filled it with gleaming gold bars. He placed it by his bedside, ready for transport.

Soon afterward, the man died and showed up at the pearly gates with his suitcase. Saint Peter greeted him and informed him that he could not allow him to bring the bag inside. The man explained that he had the Lord's permission to have one carry-on bag. Saint Peter conceded, "You can bring one carry-on bag, but I will need to check the contents before letting you through the gates." Peter opened the suitcase, wondering what could have been so precious that the man could not bear to leave it behind. "Oh," Saint Peter said in puzzlement, "I see you brought us more pavement."

Although this story is far-fetched, it holds some truth we could all heed. We may think our material possessions are of great importance, but in heaven's economy they matter little. To the rich man, his gold was precious indeed. However, in heaven it was considered only pavement.

Our Pursuit of Happiness

I enjoy beautiful things as much as anybody else. I collect porcelain dolls, and our home images the Victorian era. There is nothing wrong with enjoying the beautiful things God allows us to possess. However, we should not allow these beautiful possessions to become the center of our lives or to dictate our happiness. When I begin to focus on the wrong methods of obtaining happiness, I think so often of that song,

Jesus, You're the center of my joy;
All that's good and perfect comes from You.
You're the source of my contentment,
Hope for all I do;
Jesus, You're the center of my joy.

Jesus is the source of our contentment. Hebrews 13:5 says, "Let your conversation be without covetousness; and be content with such things as ye have: for he hath said, I will never leave thee, nor forsake thee." Our conversation should not consist of wanting more of this or that. Possessions are trivial matters. We should be content with the material blessings God has given us, but we should be aware that the ultimate contentment is that our Lord and Savior said He would never leave us nor forsake us. What a wonderful promise we have! Life may deal out some unpleasantness, but God will be there for us in spite of what we may face.

INTERVAL 3

Father Knows Best

It was a cold, winter day when I arrived home from school. To my surprise, my dad was sitting in our living room with my mom. He should have been at work because he was not due to arrive home for several more hours. By the looks on their faces, I knew something was very wrong. "Karla," Dad said, "we need to tell you what has happened today. Please come in and sit down." As the story unfolded, my quiet, secure life gradually came apart.

My dad was the postmaster in the little town in which I grew up. In fact, my dad had been born and raised there as well. The Lord had blessed him with this great job, and we as a family had enjoyed the benefits for some time. I remember telling the guys who asked for my address to simply send it to me, with the town and zip code, and I would get the letter since my dad was the postmaster. It was not necessary to include the whole address.

∞ Perspectives from a "Smart" Christian

I can still remember the despair I felt as Dad explained what happened. It appeared that someone inside his office had set him up as the fall guy. Without going into a lot of detail, some postal inspectors had arrived at his office the day after Labor Day for an inspection. Since it had been a holiday, my dad was running behind on completing the details on some packages. Because of some minor technicalities, he was "let go" to allow someone else to assume his position.

I could not believe something like that could happen in my little town. Everyone liked my dad. I just could not fathom anyone intentionally doing something to discount my dad's character. Further, I was a high school senior looking forward to the future, and this appalling event had seemingly robbed me of any chance to go to college. I remember crying so hard that my head felt like it would burst. The next day at school I could barely function because the small-town rumor mill was already churning. I am very thankful for my teachers, friends, and church family who surrounded me with their support and compassion. They lifted me and let me know they were behind my family and would do whatever they could to stand with us. A petition was circulated in support of my dad, and many people came to his defense.

Suffice it to say, it was a very difficult year for us. My wonderful dad, who had dedicated his life to the Lord and worked constantly for the church, had to start all over. His income dropped drastically because he took a job that was far beneath his capabilities. I would complain about how my dad had been betrayed by someone who supposedly was his friend and declare that he should find some way to get revenge. But my dad would always say, "That's not the right thing to do. They will have to work out their own salvation. We are responsible to God for how we react to this situation. We need to be kind to everyone and most of all keep the right spirit in spite of how we are treated."

Ironically, even though I remember the heartache, I also remember that my dad never lost his humor and his positive outlook. Yes, my senior year was not quite what I had expected, but I still remember it as being a memorable time in my life in spite of the circumstances. My dad's humor and my mom's prayers helped our family survive this devastating blow. And God was with us.

I was blessed to receive the valedictorian award and had the opportunity to speak to the audience on graduation night. I spoke of the blessings of God and how He had been with us through some difficult times. At the end of my speech, my sister played the piano while I sang "The Unseen Hand." When I started singing, I felt a peace and a calm reassurance from the Lord. I could see by the expressions on many faces that they felt it too. Through a difficult situation, God allowed my family to be a witness to our city and show them what serving God is all about. We learned to be content in spite of the circumstances.

INTERVAL 4

Smile Awhile

Philippians 4:11 says, "Not that I speak in respect of want: for I have learned, in whatsoever state I am, therewith to be content." My husband and I have had to move several times, and I do not always handle change very well. I have taken this verse of Scripture as my theme. No matter what state I am in—Texas, North Carolina, or Missouri—I am supposed to be content. Of course, I am aware that is not what the verse means, but my application of it did create some laughter in our home. It also made my husband realize how spiritual I am in my interpretation of the Scriptures.

Change is difficult, to say the least. A few years ago, my husband and I felt it was the Lord's will for us to move back to St. Louis. However, we did not realize how difficult our decision would be on our oldest daughter, Kara. She would be entering her junior year. She had developed a circle of friends in

∽ Perspectives from a "Smart" Christian

North Carolina and was not in the least interested in leaving her security. For the first couple of weeks after our move, we were very concerned because Kara did not seem to be handling the change well at all. She grieved deeply for her lost life in North Carolina. As school time neared, I noticed she became even more melancholy. The prospect of a new school and making new friends at this stage in her life just did not seem feasible.

We encouraged her to at least give our new life a chance. She agreed and assured us she would do her best. The first couple of weeks were not easy. She said everyone seemed wary of her, and she decided she needed to take action. She began to smile at everyone and begin her conversations by showing an interest in their lives. "At first," she said, "they probably thought, *What is wrong with this little short girl? All she does is smile all the time.*" But she continued to be friendly, and her smiles and kindness paid off. She had the chance to witness to several kids and brought them to church with her. During her senior year, the student body elected Kara to be their Homecoming Queen. Because of our daughter's willingness to go along with what we believed was God's will, she was blessed beyond her expectations. Since then, she has mentioned to us several times how glad she is that we moved, because so many wonderful blessings and opportunities have come her way.

Smile Awhile

A smile made the difference for Kara. A smile on many occasions has helped me break through someone's barriers of shyness or uncertainty. In fact, a smile is an excellent way to create a new look without Botox or collagen! And it has been proven by the medical community that it takes more muscles to frown than it does to smile.

A smile is a sign of contentment. A smile can also change someone's life.

My sister is a wonderful person who has a love for those born with more challenges than others. For several years, she worked with Down's syndrome children in the public school system, and they readily knew she cared about them. On numerous occasions when she and I would be at the mall, some of her students would see her and come yelling across the mall, "Hey, Miss Smart, Miss Smart." She was always ready to give them a hug and to encourage them. Even though she no longer works with these kids, they still seem to sense that she cares about them.

Recently, she and her husband entered a restaurant. As the hostess led them to a table, they passed a Down's syndrome couple who appeared to be on a date. My sister nodded to them and smiled while passing their table. When the couple got up to leave, they came straight to my sister's table. The lady said, "I just wanted to thank you so much for smiling at us. No one ever smiles at us, and I just wanted to say, 'Thank you,' because it meant so much to us."

While going through some of my notes, I noticed a statement that said, "Peace starts with a smile." Take a moment today to smile at someone. Your smile can make a difference to someone's world.

Smile awhile, and give your face a rest,
Raise your hand to the One you love the best.
Turn around to someone near,
Shake their hand, and S M I L E!

INTERVAL 5

No Fear

It was a lovely, fall day. I was on my way to the cleaners to pick up my husband's clothes so he would have them for his out-of-town trip. I drove along, thanking God for all of His blessings. The girls seemed to be adjusting to our new environment, and I felt peaceful and content.

The radio program droning in the background was suddenly interrupted by a special news broadcast. I listened in horror as the reporter described how an airplane had just crashed into one of the twin towers of the World Trade Center in New York City. By the time I arrived back home, another plane had crashed into the other tower. America now knew this was not an accident; we had been attacked.

Most everyone can describe in detail what he was doing or where he was going when he heard the news on September 11, 2001. What I remember most was the despair I felt. Just a few moments

∞ Perspectives from a "Smart" Christian

before I heard the news, I was thanking God for His peace, but it changed in just a moment's time. The beautiful and magnificent structures that took years to plan and build were destroyed in about an hour.

Several mornings after the attack, I was driving my girls to school when the 8:00 AM news report came on. The announcer began with the "bad news," which, if I remember correctly, was reporting something derogatory about the nation of Israel. In frustration, I clicked the radio off and said, "I am so sick of hearing all of this bad news. I refuse to listen any more." There was a silence in the car and then Kara asked, "But, Mom, don't you want to go to heaven?"

Good morning to me! I thought the mom was supposed to lead the children and be an example for them to follow instead of the other way around. I decided at that moment to come out of "the doldrums" and get my act together. I had been floating around in a state of anxiety and worry about the terrorist attacks, not realizing that my girls needed me to show them how to handle this tough time. We can sometimes get so caught up in "me" that we do not realize how much our family and this world need us. Kara's one statement helped me change my own perspective on the situation. My depression became hope in the Lord. I wanted to show my children not to fear and that He is our way. He will take care of us no matter what happens.

I related this incident to my very good friend,

No Fear

Phyllis Jones, and we came to a startling conclusion. We teach our children that the goal of our lives is to serve the Lord and make it to heaven. However, we try every way we can to stay right where we are. We enjoy the life that God has given us on earth so very much that we work diligently to keep our lives "as is." In the process of maintaining the status quo, we do not realize how wonderful heaven is going to be. The glory God has provided for those who love Him is beyond our wildest imagination.

A few months after my husband and I married, we had the opportunity to visit South Korea. The Elton Bernards had been kind enough to invite my husband to preach for them, and they allowed me to tag along. The trip greatly impacted my life. The Bernards had sacrificed a great deal to serve as missionaries to this land. But in spite of their sacrifice and the struggles they endured, I remember the humor that was also a part of their lives. They handled everything as if it were no big deal.

One aspect of the trip I remember was the driving procedures. It reminded me of little bugs scurrying to and fro. The cars would make four lanes into six lanes and drive furiously. To say the least, I clung to the door handles and developed a prayer life like I had never had before. Elder Bernard did not let any of this affect him. He entered the traffic flow and drove just like the rest of them. I am certain he heard my back-seat hissing and slamming on my invisible brake, for he would turn around, grin, and say, "It's okay, Sis. God is with us." I already knew God was with us. But I was wondering if He was with the rest of the drivers!

While there, we also had the opportunity to be with the William Turner family. They had recently arrived in South Korea, and I marveled at their upbeat, positive attitude. I remember how excited their two children were when we spent the night with them in their apartment because we were from home. Even though things were difficult and living in the land of their calling was not an easy task, these families provided us with much laughter and memories for a lifetime.

Following our time there, the Bernards returned to America on furlough and brought along two or three of the national pastors. My husband saw Elder Bernard at a conference and asked him how things were going. He said the national pastors were awed by our American malls, restaurants, and homes. One of the national pastors had made the comment that America was how he envisioned heaven would be: wonderful sites, the accessibility of anything imaginable, and the best of everything right within reach.

Perhaps the good life we have in America keeps us from realizing the wonderful place God has prepared for us. The attack on our land, however, helps me realize how vulnerable we are and how dispensable material things are. We have magnificent structures, historical monuments of great significance, and beautiful cities and towns across our land. But just like the World Trade Center, they could be gone within a few moments' time.

However, God does not want us to live under the bondage of fear. I John 4:18 says, "There is no fear in love; but perfect love casteth out fear: because fear hath torment. He that feareth is not made perfect in love."

A few years ago, America embraced the slogan "No Fear." God wants us to "fear not," but He also wants us to be aware of the snares of the enemy. II Timothy 1:7 reiterates, "For God hath not given us the spirit of fear; but of power, and of love, and of a sound mind." We "fear" God, but we should have no fear when it comes to things of this world and the wiles of the devil.

When I was little girl, my dad, mom, and Danita Sudderth, a lady in our church, sang a song that often floats across my memory: "Too Much to Gain to Lose." (This perhaps could also serve as a reason for not dieting, but I will not go that route at this time.) One line in the song says "And defeat is one word I don't use." How often I have repeated that line! Defeat is failing to get up again when one is knocked down. No matter what life tries to bury us with, we can rise above the rubble and debris. We may be down, but we are not going to stay down. "I'll be up again; just you wait and see." (Excuse my

◯ Perspectives from a "Smart" Christian

constant referral to lines from songs that seem to come to mind. However, my spirituality is affirmed again, for the Book of Isaiah tells me to "make sweet melody, sing many songs, that [I] mayest be remembered." I am just doing as the Bible instructs. I am singing many songs. And most of all, I will be remembered. Wow! What a promise! I again found the good.)

Too many sunsets lie behind the mountain;
Too many rivers my feet have walked through.
Too many treasures are waiting over yonder;
I've got too much to gain to lose.

—Dottie Rambo

INTERVAL 6

Still Crazy after All These Years

My telephone rings and how thankful I am for that wonderful caller-ID mechanism. I reach for the phone with anticipation as it shows the caller to be my sister, Vicki. I always look forward to talking with Vicki because she will either have news of some kind or will have some tidbit to share that will bring laughter to my day.

"Hey, Karla, what are you doing?" she always asks.

"Not a whole lot," is usually my answer. "What are you doing?" (I know you are much impressed with this in-depth conversation, but just be patient. It will get better.)

"Well," she responds, "I'm listening to my theme song."

"And what theme song might that be?" I ask.

"Oh, I think you will remember it," she says. "Remember that song we listened to as kids, 'Still Crazy after All These Years'? I have decided that I am going to adopt that as my theme song."

I'm thinking, *How like Vicki to come up with something that makes me laugh.* And yes, she has brought much laughter to our family through the years with her craziness and humor. I am using Vicki as an example in this chapter because she deserves her day to shine.

I called Vicki today to get a little background information, and I informed her of my intentions to include some things about her in my book.

"So you're writing a book, are you?" she asked as I explained my reason for calling. "Well, if that is the case, you can just leave my chapter out." Of course, as you may surmise, we had a good laugh together.

Vicki is a wonderful person who has been a special part of my life since I was old enough to be aware she existed in my world. My mother told me that on the day I arrived home from the hospital, Vicki had my best interests at heart. Mom laid me on the couch in a nest of pillows and told little Vicki to stay close to me for a few minutes while she got settled in. When Mom came back, she heard smacking noises and saw Vicki bending over me. She rushed to see what Vicki was doing. My dear, wonderful sister was holding a caramel candy at my mouth, and I was licking vigorously at this wonderful taste. Of course, Mom quickly took away this delectable treat and told Vicki that I could not yet eat candy. However, my sister only had my best interests at heart.

On many occasions, Vicki bought me cherry cokes with the money she earned from her job as a soda jerk at Rose Drugstore. Now, I know her job title does not sound very impressive, but I thought she had a wonderful position. I would go to the drugstore, and she would concoct for me all kinds of exquisite ice cream dishes: hot fudge sundaes, banana splits, and coke floats.

When Vicki learned to drive, she would take me to "drag main." And when she bought that teal Cutlass Supreme with the white, soft-padded half-top with the money she earned from teaching piano—well, I thought we had indeed arrived! No longer did we have to use the family car as our mode of transportation. Vicki now had a snazzy set of wheels we could be proud to motor around in.

I was quite sad when Vicki moved to Lubbock, Texas, to assist with the music ministry there. My transportation came to a halt, and the laughter and fun I had taken for granted were several hundred miles removed. However, I always tried to have a good spirit and somehow recovered from the loss.

Vicki and I were known as the "Smart sisters" in the Texico District. We heard a lot of comments about our last name, such as, "You may think you're smart, and you really are!" We took the teasing in good stride. To be honest, we rather enjoyed being "smart."

God blessed Vicki with much musical talent. She

could play the piano and organ superbly. She even took time to teach me, the younger sister, a few musical techniques, although I never quite reached her level of expertise. She played for Texico camps from the time she was about sixteen and made her talent available to anyone who might need it.

My husband and I began dating, and because we sometimes wanted to go by ourselves, Vicki was often thrown into the company of Mark's brother, Joe. It turned out that Joe and Vicki got married before Mark and I did! My older sister married Mark's younger brother. The Smart sisters married the Christian brothers. You can imagine the jokes we heard then. "You used to be smart but now you're a Christian." (Perhaps now you understand more clearly the title of my book.)

I admire and love my sister, not just for her kindness to me but also for the many struggles she has faced in her life and the way she has handled those struggles.

She served as music minister for Rex Johnson for several years. At the age of 38, she was diagnosed with rheumatoid arthritis. This is a difficult, painful disease for anyone but even more so for a musician. Vicki began the long journey of trying to find the medication that would best alleviate the symptoms. I do not know how many times the doctors have changed her medicine or her treatments. I do know that it has been a difficult time for Vicki.

Still Crazy after All These Years

Unfortunately, she had to give up her position as music minister. I remember calling her on Monday following a Sunday service, and she could hardly get around because of the effort she had put forth on Sunday. Yet she still tried to continue serving in spite of her struggle. And she still continues to serve as secretary at Christian Life Church in Austin, Texas.

During our telephone conversations, very rarely does she mention her illness. If she does, it is usually in a joking manner about having a stiff neck and that she needs prayer that God will help her get her nose out of the air because of her stiff neck. She mentioned once that she seemed only to be able to look forward, that she could turn neither to the right nor to the left.

Yet she keeps going. I know some days she has difficulty getting around, but she says she does much better when she is out and around other people.

I appreciate the attitude that Vicki displays on a daily basis. I feel that her positive attitude has kept her doing as well as she has. While she could just plop down in that easy chair and let life pass her by, she chooses to continue to work for the Lord in other ways. And yes, she continues to play the organ for church services. Her music has been her life, and she continues to share it with others.

So, Vicki, I did not honor your request and leave out your chapter. I feel that your life is a living example of what having a positive outlook is all about.

∽ Perspectives from a "Smart" Christian

You are an overcomer! You continue to find the good things in life. You may still be "Crazy after All These Years," but your sister is so glad you are!

INTERVAL 7

The Joy of Children

Motherhood is something to which most young girls aspire. I remember my youthful desire to have a husband, raise wonderful children, and change the world with my knowledge and wisdom. However, being a mother brought more surprises and challenges than I ever imagined.

The Lord blessed us with three delightful daughters who have added much joy to our lives. On occasion, however, the joy is not always evident. It is not always a picture-perfect family that resides within the walls of our home. There are bad days: the fussing, making messes, complaining, and whining. You know the routines. One such joyous day occurred following the birth of our third daughter, Kalee. My husband was out of town, and on this particular day my three munchkins had almost driven me crazy. I could not wait to get them all in bed. Kalee had colic, Kara was whiny, and Courtney was trashing everything.

❧ Perspectives from a "Smart" Christian

I finally had had it. "Come on," I said short-temperedly. "Everyone to bed, now!"

"Can't we pray?" Courtney asked hesitantly.

"Okay," I said, suddenly becoming quite spiritual (not). "Let's pray." (I'm certain from the tone of my voice that the Lord was really looking forward to hearing my prayer.)

Three-year-old Courtney said, "I'll pray tonight." Fine. Great. I was too tired to pray anyway.

"Jesus, we love You," she began. "Pease bless my mommy. Her's so tired and weary. And Jesus, pease help my mommy to enjoy her three children."

Well, needless to say, I felt small enough to sit on a curb and swing my feet. My children can so innocently remind me of the important things in life. All I wanted to do at that time was get them in bed so I could have a moment to myself. Instead, Courtney prayed that I would learn to enjoy my children.

We want our kids to be the prettiest, the smartest, and the best behaved. If I could pinpoint one of my faults (most of the time, they are too numerous to number), it would be that I judge a situation and take action before allowing further investigation. Many times I wish I could take back words I have said or actions I have taken. Instead, I have jumped headlong into a situation with my kids and later learned it was not what it appeared.

I heard a cute story about a mother who entered

her daughter's empty bedroom and saw a letter addressed to herself propped up on the desk. With shaking hands, she unfolded the letter and began to read:

"It is with great regret that I'm telling you I have eloped with my boyfriend. I know you are upset, but I know you want me to be happy. I have found real love. I am fascinated by his tattoos and piercings, and I just love his big motorcycle.

"Another thing. I'm pregnant. But don't worry; Ahmed said we will be very happy in his trailer in the swamp. And he wants more children.

"I've also learned that drugs aren't really that bad for you and that selling them is quite profitable. It will support us well.

"Don't worry, Mom; I'm fifteen years old and I do know how to take care of myself. Someday I will come back to visit because you will want to get to know your grandchild.

Love, Judith

"P.S. Mom, the above is not true. I'm over at Sarah's house. I just wanted to show you that there are worse things in life than the school report card that's in my desk. Love ya!"

∞ Perspectives from a "Smart" Christian

How funny yet how true this is! While writing this chapter, I am "preaching" to myself. I tend to look for the bad before I see the good that is so apparent. It is all in how we interpret a situation.

Another favorite story of mine is about a little boy who went with his mom to the YWCA for her exercise class. As they walked into the dressing room, several women were in the process of changing clothes, and they all began shrieking, grabbing for towels, and running when they noticed the little boy in the room. With his child-like innocence, he looked up at his mother and asked, "Mommy, what's wrong with these ladies? Have they never seen a little boy before?"

Early this week during my morning ritual, I reached to retrieve the hairspray can from beneath my bathroom sink. Much to my dismay, the can was not in its proper place. So, being the good and kind mother that I am, I became somewhat irate and began expounding on the trial of never finding the hairspray when I need it. The girls know not to take the hairspray. Why do they continually ignore my instructions and take it anyway? It creates such an inconvenience for me! Enter their father. He peered at me while I was expounding on my struggle and then quietly said, "You know, someday you are going to wish the girls were here to take your hairspray."

Well, hello to me! Not only do my children have words of wisdom for me, but my husband also shares

The Joy of Children

his words of admonition in such a quiet, calm manner. And, blam! Such truth he imparts! (Don't you hate it when you realize someone else is so right?)

But he is so right! That missing bottle of hairspray is just a minor inconvenience. Instead, I should think about the times the hairspray is in its proper place. I should think of the times that the girls have so willingly helped clean the house just because they know I like things neat. I should think about the prayers they have prayed for me when I was very sick and they had the faith to believe God would heal me. I should focus on the good things they do instead of getting upset about a misplaced hairspray bottle.

Don't allow stresses, pressures, and frustrations rob you of the joy you can find through your family. Look for the good in your children before you automatically assume the bad.

INTERVAL 8

Too Much to Do

My nephew, Geoffrey, sat in his Sunday school kindergarten class, coloring the activity for the lesson. He raised his hand, and the teacher acknowledged the signal. "Yes, Geoff, what did you need?"

"I need to use the restroom," Geoff responded.

The teacher, thinking he was just trying to find an excuse to leave the class, said, "Well, Geoffrey, class is almost over, and I think you could probably wait a couple more minutes so we don't have to interrupt things. Just finish your paper."

Reluctantly, he again picked up his crayon and started coloring. He scribbled for a few minutes and then put the crayon on the table. "Are you finished, Geoff?" the teacher asked.

"No, ma'am," he replied. "It's just hard to work when you're under pressure."

How well we can identify! When stress and pressure

❧ Perspectives from a "Smart" Christian

surround us, they inhibit our productivity. We can become so overwhelmed with all the "to dos" that it is difficult to focus on completing just one task.

I read about a woman who telephoned a friend and asked how she was feeling. "Terrible," came the reply over the wire. "My head's splitting, and my back and legs are killing me. The house is a mess, and the kids are simply driving me crazy." Very sympathetically the caller said, "Listen, go and lie down. I'll come over right away and cook lunch for you, clean up the house, and take care of the children while you get some rest. By the way, how is Sam?"

"Sam?" the complaining housewife gasped. "I have no husband named Sam."

"My heavens!" exclaimed the first woman. "I must have dialed the wrong number."

There was a long pause, and then the harried mother asked hopefully, "Are you still coming over?"

Yes, there are times we would gladly accept help from anybody—anybody at all. We are so overwhelmed that any amount of help would be appreciated. The to-do list seems to grow longer and longer by the minute.

One night I was dwelling on the many tasks that needed to be completed. I had asked the girls several times to go to bed. I knew that I had not given them the attention they deserved, but these "to dos" just seemed too important at the time. We had company coming and I wanted everything to be just right. While I was distracted, they continued to play and delay their bedtime. Finally, realizing they had not followed my instructions, I got upset and gave them a lecture about how important it was to mind Mommy because I had so much on my mind and could not deal with them right now. Quiet and subdued, they walked out of the room with their heads down. Still, I was so focused on the "to dos" that I didn't notice their sadness.

After about thirty minutes, I heard a hesitant knock on my door. Frustrated, I pulled the door open and found Kara standing there. "Now what?" I asked.

"Nothing, Mommy," she said quietly. "I just wanted to tell you that I love you before I go to sleep." Needless to say, the "to dos" suddenly seemed insignificant.

How often does the Lord feel like Kara? He stands patiently, waiting on us to spend time with Him. He waits and waits while we complete our to-do list and then hopes we will commune with Him. Yet after we complete the to-do list, we are too tired to talk with Him. All He wants to do is to tell us that He loves us.

While a teenager, I remember listening to the song "I Miss My Time with You." It said, "I miss my time with you, those moments together. I want to be with you each day, but it hurts me when you say you're too busy." I want to be cognizant of spending time with Jesus. I don't want to miss my time with Him.

We balance our family, our home, and our church,

trying to make precious time count. But the most productive, healing, and cleansing time you will spend is with Jesus. Do not let the to-do list or the pressures of this world rob you of your ultimate strength. Let's not neglect or rush our time with Him.

I miss My time with you,
Those moments together.
I want to be with you each day,
But it hurts Me when you say
You're too busy,
Busy trying to serve Me.
But how can you serve Me
When your spirit's empty?
There's a longing in My heart
Wanting more than just a part of you;
It's true,
I miss My time with you.

—LARNELLE HARRIS AND PHILL MCHUGH

INTERVAL 9

Touching the Lives of Others

Family prayer time is not always easy to organize. One night it had been a bit difficult to gather all the kids, complete the bedtime preparations, and then kneel together in prayer. However, we finally got it together and were kneeling in the girls' room. Courtney again wanted to pray. (She always seemed to be the spiritual one.) She began, "I love you, Jesus. Please forgive me of my sins. Touch Grandpa and Grandma, touch Mommy and Daddy, touch Nanaw and Papaw, touch Aunt Vicki, Uncle Joe, Shanna and Geoffrey, touch . . . touch . . . touch . . ." (long pause). Then peering out from behind her little hands, she said, "It's so hard to know who to touch sometimes."

Yes, it is hard to keep up with all the needs and problems of those around us. We are aware that there are those who need their lives "touched" more than others. However, Courtney had the concept right. We just keep trying to touch all of the lives we encounter on a daily basis while asking for God's wisdom.

When we moved to St. Louis, Courtney was entering the eighth grade. She was affected by our move but didn't seem to mind it as much as Kara. Courtney has the type of personality that enables her to find a way to make any situation work. She made friends and began bringing them to church. We would pick up the girls for church and then take them with us to eat out. One of the young ladies received the Holy Ghost and seemed to be doing well.

However, one night Courtney got a call from her saying she didn't think she wanted to be in the church any longer because she couldn't do some things. She felt like she was missing out on so much. Well, to say the least, Courtney was devastated by her friend's decision. She felt she had poured so much into her friend, but nothing had mattered. For several months, she couldn't seem to get past the thought that she had somehow failed in her attempt to win someone to God.

I was concerned for her, so I spoke to some of our friends about the situation. Jason Sciscoe, an evangelist friend, said something that helped Courtney a great deal. He said that sometimes the enemy will put those seeming failures in our lives to distract us from winning others to the Lord. We can become so focused on why they didn't stay in church that we overlook others who really want to find God. Courtney took the advice and began looking for others who were hungry for God.

That is when she met Amy, a girl in one of Courtney's classes. Courtney began making friends with Amy and started inviting her to church. At first Amy was not sure about Courtney, but she agreed to come to church. Thankfully, the Lord made a wonderful change in Amy's life. She was filled with His Spirit and baptized in His wonderful name. I was overwhelmed once again with the saving power of God when I heard Amy's testimony. She drank and was beginning to experiment with drugs. She had thought of taking her own life because of the emptiness she felt. But she had noticed that Courtney was always happy and friendly and that she cared about others. She sensed there was something different about Courtney and wanted to check it out. She has been doing well in serving God, all because Courtney decided to reach out and touch the life of someone else.

It may be hard to know whom to touch. But God knows. We have the opportunity to touch so many lives on a daily basis. We cannot be distracted if someone is not as receptive as we had hoped. We need to keep believing that God will lead us to those who are hungry for a change, to those who are hurting and desire to be touched by His love.

Perspectives from a "Smart" Christian

Touching Jesus is all that really matters,
Then your life will never be the same;
There is only one way to touch Him,
Just believe when you call on His name.

—JOHN STALLINGS

INTERVAL 10

One of Those Bad Days

Women are emotional creatures (just ask any man). We tend to operate by the senses. We're affected by what we see, hear, smell, feel, and taste. I am really affected by what I taste, especially if it is cheesecake. A good piece of cheesecake makes me really happy.

A dear friend of mine was experiencing a rather difficult day. She called and wanted to go to lunch. When we sat to order, she said, "I'll take your juiciest cheeseburger with fries, and I'll follow that with a hot-fudge brownie. As you can tell," she continued, "I'm having a bad day." It was humorous and we laughed about it.

Yes, we all have our bad days. When I have one of those days, I like to think about something funny or maybe read a good book that will bring a little laughter to my life. The key is to look for something good in every situation, to be positive.

∞ Perspectives from a "Smart" Christian

So perhaps you are having a bad day. You may feel like the world is against you. A few years ago, Courtney was in the process of working on an important English composition based on the book *Gone with the Wind*. She asked me to proofread. As I read her conclusion, I could not help but laugh. In the final statement, she wrote, "My opinion of this book is simply that all the characters had to live in a doggy-dog world." I asked her, "Court, exactly what does this statement mean?" She answered, "Oh, Mom, you know. I have heard you and Dad use the same words. It's when everyone is out to get everyone else." She had the right concept but the wrong words.

It seems at times that everyone is just out for himself. He does not bother to make certain someone else is okay; he just makes sure that everything in his corner of the world is fine. As Christians, we cannot afford to live "doggy-dog" lives, thinking only of ourselves. We must project our thoughts beyond ourselves, even when we are having a bad day.

How a person handles discouragement will show what kind of person she really is. How we react in the bad times will bring out what is inside our hearts.

We face stress and challenges daily. It is not easy to obtain joy from or to see the good in every situation. Perhaps we may feel like three-year-old Kalee did a few years ago after she had misbehaved rather severely. I sent her to her room for a time-out. Since it was quiet in her room and that is not one of her

One of Those Bad Days

characteristics, I became concerned and decided to peek through the door. I saw her sitting on her bed with one of those old-fashioned chalkboard erasers. She was rubbing it all over her face and body, while chalk particles filled the air. With satisfaction in her voice, she said, "See, I am no longer here." Boy, I wish life came with an eraser. Wouldn't it be nice to erase ourselves out of every bad situation? But we know it is not that easy and certainly not possible. So what do we do?

I don't mean to brag, but women are amazing. They bear hardships and they carry burdens, but they hold happiness, love, and joy. They have the opportunity to influence so much in our world. I do not think we really realize how powerful an influence we can be. We influence our children, and we can even change our husbands' minds (look at Eve). My girls often make the statement, "If Mom ain't happy, no one is happy." Of course, I realize they are just giving me a hard time, but we really do have a powerful effect on our families. God made us that way.

As a minister's wife, I realized I could affect many things in the church. Confession time: I'm not always as spiritual as I should be. One day, unfortunately, I was in a whiny mode because only a few people in the church we pastored showed up for what should have been a very big project. So I began to murmur and complain: "They don't love us here. All they care

༄ Perspectives from a "Smart" Christian

about are their lives and making themselves happy. I just feel like we're servants here. That's all we are—just servants."

Well, my husband kindly and quietly brought me back to the reality of our purpose. He said, "A servant is the greatest in the kingdom. We should want to be servants of God." I just hate it when my husband does that! He is so good at quoting the Bible to me, just when I don't really need it. Here I was enjoying my bad day, and he had to remind me that we were honored to be servants of God. Perhaps there should be a verse of Scripture that says, "Blame them that have the rule over you," instead of, "Obey them that have the rule over you."

God tells us that He wants us to be happy and enjoy life. John 15:11 says, "These things have I spoken unto you, that my joy might remain in you, and that your joy might be full." I realize that not every day is going to be "hunky dory." You will have bad days or down times. Just remember that God knows exactly where you are. I once heard a statement that said, "When you get to your wit's end, you'll find God there." That is a fact of life.

On those bad days, think on the good things of God. Get out of the doldrums. Look around at God's blessings and, most of all, give thanks for His goodness. You will be amazed at how much better things will appear if you just take a minute to regroup and look for the good.

One of Those Bad Days

Because you have an occasional spell of despondency, do not despair. After all, remember that the sun has a sinking spell every night, but rises again in the morning.

—L&N Magazine

INTERVAL 11

Don't Let the Grouches Get You Down

I received an e-mail recently that offered several tips on "How to Stay Young." Included in that list was, "Keep only cheerful friends. The grouches pull you down." That is so true! I can think of people whom I enjoy being around, but I can also think of a few folks whom I try to avoid because of their dour attitudes and outlook on life.

My husband and I had the privilege of assisting J. T. Pugh for a few years. We learned so much under the Pughs' leadership, and we will always cherish the time we spent with them. In one of his masterpiece sermons, he made a statement that had a great impact on me. He said, "I know that God loves me, but I want God to like me." Yes, we know beyond a shadow of a doubt that God loves us, because He died for us. However, what would we have to do to make God like us?

I have thought about that often. Perhaps God

⌒ Perspectives from a "Smart" Christian

would like to be around someone who has a joyful attitude. He would like someone who did not begrudge serving Him. And He would like someone who is nice to others. He does not want a bunch of "grump muffins" in heaven.

Psychologists have long wondered what motivates people to be nice. Researchers from Emory University have found that cooperating with another person activates the pleasure centers of the brain. They also found that most women who chose to work together responded much better to games and activities. Neurologist Gregory Burns said, "This suggests that people find it rewarding to cooperate with each other. Mutual small acts of kindness really do make you feel better."

The Bible instructs us that it is much better to give than to receive. I think this refers to more than monetary substance. We should do our best to show kindness to everyone around us. We should make it easy for folks to get along with us. We should be nice. How many times did I hear that as a child?

We do not want to be like the little boy who was overheard praying, "Lord, if You can't make me a better boy, don't worry about it. I'm having a real good time just like I am."

In my home church, most everyone seemed to have trouble getting along with one particular lady. It seemed everyone dreaded talking to her because she usually would find something derogatory to say.

Don't Let the Grouches Get You Down

As a little girl, I tried to avoid her because she frightened me. However, my sister always tried to be kind to her. The woman was not always kind in return, but Vicki made an effort to extend kindness anyway. There came a time when Vicki was struggling, needing some answers. This lady came up to Vicki one night and said, "I have a verse of Scripture for you." She referred her to Psalm 37:4-5: "Delight thyself also in the Lord; and he shall give thee the desires of thine heart. Commit thy way unto the Lord; trust also in him; and he shall bring it to pass." I never saw changes in the lady's actions, but she did help Vicki find the answers she needed.

I realize that each of us has her own personality and her own inhibitions. But we should try to make kindness a part of our lives. When you feel out of sorts or grumpy, make an effort to be nice. Don't be a grouch. I do not think the Lord likes a grouch, and remember that we want the Lord not only to love us but also to like us.

Kindness makes a fellow feel good, whether it's being done to him or by him.
—Frank A. Clark

INTERVAL 12

The Best Response

During a science class, a teacher was discussing whales. A little girl raised her hand and told the story about Jonah and the whale. After she finished, the teacher said that it was physically impossible for a whale to swallow a human because even though it was a very large mammal, its throat was very small. The little girl emphatically repeated that the whale swallowed Jonah. Irritated, the teacher reiterated that a whale could not swallow a human. It was physically impossible. The little girl said, "Well, when I get to heaven I will just ask Jonah." The teacher responded, "What if Jonah went to hell?" To which the little girl replied, "Then you can ask him."

Children never hesitate to tell it like it is. They are not afraid to share any information, especially something they have overheard from Mom or Dad. Children seldom misquote you. In fact, they usually repeat word for word what you say. And they may

◠ Perspectives from a "Smart" Christian

add their own commentary, just to make the story more interesting. Children do not intend to be mean or unkind. They simply take things literally and see a given situation as black or white.

As an adult, I am a bit more cautious with my actions and comments. I will talk around an issue to try to convince someone rather than just hitting them full-force with the truth. I believe it is better first to present the positive side of an issue before discussing the negative side.

My husband is quite an expert at presenting the best side first. If something unplanned or unfortunate happens in our family, he will immediately begin talking about the positive things first before he lets me know the bad side of the situation. However, after twenty-five years of marriage, I think perhaps I have learned his game plan. Our girls have also picked up on his maneuvers.

A few weeks ago, I was upstairs preparing for bed. I knew the girls would be arriving home anytime and that Mark was downstairs waiting on them. I heard a loud crash that seemed to shake the house, so I ran to the top of the stairs and yelled, "Is everything all right?" There was a slight pause, and my husband answered, "Yes, babe, everything's fine." I sat and started reading my book again. In a few minutes, Kalee came into the room and said, "How you doing, Mom?" I could tell by her face that something was not quite right. "I'm fine, Kalee," I answered. "Is

The Best Response

everything okay?" "Sure, Mom," she answered, "everything's fine."

In a few minutes, she came back in my room singing a song. She sat a few minutes and then went out of the room again. I was getting more and more suspicious. Again, she came back in the room. "Kalee, what is going on?" I asked. "What are Kara and Dad doing?" "Oh, nothing," she said. "They are just talking about insurance." There was my clue! I knew something had happened.

I was putting on my robe when Mark walked into the room. "Is everything all right?" I asked him. "Oh, yes, things are okay. Babe, you know that freezer of ours has about seen its day. We probably need to see about getting another one, don't you think?"

"Okay, what has happened?" I asked Mark. "Well," he said in his long, slow drawl, "Kara just had a little accident as she was pulling into the garage. Her foot slipped on the accelerator, and she ran into the freezer. But that old freezer wasn't that great. We probably need a new one anyway."

Do you see how my family works together to hide things from me? It is the greatest cover-up of the century. But at least they present the good side first to cushion the negative side of things. They have learned it from the best negotiator—their dad.

My girls attended a Christian school for the first few elementary grades. However, when we moved to North Carolina, we decided to put them in public

☙ Perspectives from a "Smart" Christian

school. I was a bit concerned because they had not yet had to explain their beliefs, so I gave them some advice on how to handle the situation. I told them if they were questioned about their skirts, they should simply tell the other kids that their parents thought it was better for girls to be ladies and that wearing skirts was an indication of being a little lady. Then when they got to know everybody and made friends, they could explain it in more detail. One morning at breakfast, nine-year-old Kara said, "Mommy, I did what you told me about answering the other kids' questions, and they thought that was so cool." Six-year-old Courtney spoke up: "Well, I didn't answer their questions that way. I just told them I was Pentecostal and that was the way we believed." "Oh," I said, "and what did they say?" Courtney shrugged and said, "They didn't say much, but they haven't asked me anything else." Well, okay then. They handled the situation differently but came up with the same result.

Late one night I was working on a project for Word Aflame. Kalee was about three years old, and I had asked her several times to go to bed. She kept assuring me she was not sleepy. I glanced at her, and it looked like she had fallen asleep. Frustrated because she would not go to bed, I asked, "Kalee, are you asleep?" With eyes completely shut and not even raising her head, she said, "No, Mommy, I'm just trying to give you a little peace."

The Best Response

That is what we all hope for, a peaceful resolution. Life will hand us some interesting dilemmas. We choose how we will respond. The little girl knew she was right about the story of Jonah. She believed it so emphatically that she thought the teacher would go to hell because she did not believe the Word of God. However, perhaps she did not choose the best way to respond to the teacher.

That is where we can be helpful. I am comforted to know that my girls are watching my husband and me and are learning the best way to approach their struggles. Of course, my husband is much better at finding a solution than I am. The girls do seem to be learning that the best response is to have a positive attitude until a peaceful solution or answer can be found.

As the sun creates your shadow, God creates your soul—but in each case, it is you who determines the shape of it.

—Frank A. Clark

INTERVAL 13

Finding Gladness

I grew up in the small town of Farwell, Texas, population 1035. As one might presume, the town was lacking in the field of entertainment. I spent a good portion of my time with my head stuck in a book. When I ran out of Nancy Drew mysteries, I turned to the Hardy Boys. However, I much preferred reading books about heroines instead of heroes.

To create a diversion in my bookish existence, my parents purchased a long-play album, or what I called a "record," entitled *Pollyanna*. I listened to that record over and over. Pollyanna was a little girl raised by missionary parents, but when they died, she was brought to live with her rich Aunt Polly. Pollyanna had lived with few earthly possessions and in sparse and primitive surroundings, and she wore hand-me-down clothes. In spite of this, she always found something to be happy about. She used to play a game called the "Glad Game." If something made her unhappy, she would immediately find something to be glad about.

She met many interesting people: Nancy, who did not like her job; Angelica, the grumpy housemaid who tired of Pollyanna's constant bright chatter; Mrs. Snow, an invalid lady who certainly enjoyed her poor health; and Reverend Ford, the minister who catered to Aunt Polly's whims. Pollyanna played her Glad Game with all of these people. When Aunt Polly did not seem to be enjoying her wealth, Pollyanna told her, "You should be glad, for you're so very rich."

Pollyanna visited Mrs. Snow when others avoided her at all costs. She taught her the Glad Game by telling her she could be glad about being in bed because it gave her a chance to view all the pretty rainbows the sun made on her wall. When Angelica and Nancy talked of dreading Sundays because of Reverend Ford's fire-and-brimstone sermons, she reminded them that they should be glad because they had roast chicken and wonderful cakes to eat on Sunday.

Then one day she delivered Aunt Polly's desired message to Reverend Ford and introduced him to the "happy texts" of the Bible. She told him there were eight hundred happy texts. She said, "If God took the trouble to tell us eight hundred times to be glad and rejoice, then He must have meant it."

At the end of the story, she fell from a tree and was badly injured. The whole town came to see her and played her own Glad Game with her. Her positive attitude had changed a small, better-than-thou town into a town that started caring and wanting to give. She taught them to be glad and to look for the good in everything. They even changed the name of their town to Glad Town.

Abraham Lincoln made the statement, "If you look for the bad in mankind, you will surely find it." If we always expect to see the bad side of people, we will overlook their goodness. The same is true with life in general. We usually get out of life what we expect or what we are looking for.

Deuteronomy 28:45, 47 says, "Moreover all these curses shall come upon thee, and shall pursue thee, and overtake thee, till thou be destroyed; because thou hearkenedst not unto the voice of the Lord thy God, to keep his commandments and his statutes which he commanded thee. . . . Because thou servedst not the Lord thy God with joyfulness, and with gladness of heart, for the abundance of all things."

What an eye-opening Scripture setting! This gives an explanation for the reason some of the curses came upon the Israelites. They were not serving God with gladness. If we are just keeping the commandments but not serving God with gladness and joy in our hearts, we are not serving God the way He desires. It is God's will for us to have joyful hearts while serving Him, but He wants us to

◠ Perspectives from a "Smart" Christian

serve Him because we want to and not because we have to.

A little boy was restless in a church service. His mother admonished him over and over to be still and sit. Finally, she reached over and physically sat him in the pew. After a few seconds, he looked at her and whispered, "I may be sitting down on the outside, but I'm still standing up on the inside." He was doing what his mother desired, but he certainly did not want to.

When I think of what God has given me, my heart overflows with gratefulness. He gave His life for me that I might live an abundant life in Him. In spite of all the sacrifices He made, He still wants me to be glad about serving Him. Psalm 126:3 says, "The LORD hath done great things for us; whereof we are glad."

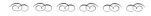

I can be glad for my hope is in the Lord,
'Cause He gives a confidence that this world
doesn't know.
He's the Lord of all creation,
And whatever the situation
I'm glad for my hope's in the Lord.

—LARNELLE HARRIS

INTERVAL 14

Share the Joy

A song I enjoyed singing as a child was "Jesus Is Mine." I remember how I enjoyed emphasizing the *mine* word. It went something like this:

Mine, mine, mine,
Jesus is mine.
Mine when I'm weary,
Mine when I'm cheery.
Mine, mine, mine,
Jesus is mine.
Mine all the time, He is mine!

It reminds me of a child in an argument yelling, "That's mine!" Perhaps that's why I remember the tune and the words so well. I said the word so much, I thought it was neat that I could say the word in church. I do not mean to cast a negative reflection on the song, because I realize the composer simply wanted Jesus in his life. However, we should want others to have Jesus, instead of keeping Him to ourselves.

Proverbs 11:30 says, "The fruit of the righteous is a tree of life; and he that winneth souls is wise." In Philippians 2:14-17, Paul saw us as "lights in the world; holding forth the word of life," and said, "I joy, and rejoice with you all." There are wisdom and joy in soulwinning.

What is the greatest thing we can do to influence others for Jesus? Answer: live in such a way that others watching our lives will say, "I don't know what that person has, but I want some of it." The loudest message we preach is the life we live before others.

In His Word, God tells us that He wants us to be happy and enjoy life. John 15:11 says, "These things have I spoken unto you, that my joy might remain in you, and that your joy might be full." Our God wants us to be joyful, for if we exude joy, it will make others want what we have. We can be an example to those around us by showing a joyful and glad attitude.

Courtney returned home from a conference she was privileged to attend due to her academic awards. She met many other young people and served on the National Youth Leadership Council. Of course, they noticed she was different. However, she went out of her way to be friendly to everyone and showed the joy of the Lord through her smile and

Share the Joy

laughter. One of her roommates was a young lady from Iowa. She told Courtney that she knew a couple of other girls who were Pentecostal. However, she said they did not act like Courtney. She was surprised that Courtney acted the way she did and belonged to the same religion.

The kids exchanged notes, and I got to read some of what they wrote about Courtney. One said, "You're awesome! Your energy and personality uplifted and provided fun and humor for the whole group. Veronica."

Another said, "Dearest Courtney, I'm so glad I was able to get to know you. You have opened my eyes to understand many things, especially your religion. You are very strong in your viewpoints but still listen to what other people have to say. Please keep in touch! Julie."

Others also made nice comments concerning her laughter and humor. My point is that Courtney's joy and friendliness helped people recognize that she was approachable and fun and that her religion did not inhibit her or cause her to withdraw from the group.

Maya Angelou wrote, "I've learned that people will forget what you said, people will forget what you did, but people will never forget how you made them feel."

One day a little girl was watching her mother do the dishes at the kitchen sink. She suddenly noticed that her mother had several strands of white hair in contrast to her brown hair. She inquisitively asked,

◠ Perspectives from a "Smart" Christian

"Mommy, why are some of your hairs white?" Her mom replied, "Well, every time you do something wrong or make me sad or unhappy, one of my hairs turns white. Right now you have brought so much joy to my life that most of my hair is still brown." The little girl thought for a minute and then said, "Momma, how come all of Grandma's hairs are white?"

We have access to the most wonderful gift—the Holy Ghost—that gives us the capacity to live a joyful life. We can choose to be joyful. We can radiate the joy of the Lord to those in our circle of influence. We should go out of our way to be friendly to those who do not have the truth. Our joy should shine through us as lights to this world.

The surest mark of a Christian is not faith or even love, but joy.

—SAMUEL SHOEMAKER

INTERVAL 15

The Power of Words

A conversation I overheard while with my daughter Kara makes me realize once again how things can change through the years. Certain words take on brand-new meanings. I heard someone say to her, "Kara, you are so fat!" To which she replied, "Thank you so much." When we walked away, I said, "Kara, I can't believe they said that to you. You're not fat!" Laughingly she replied, "Mom, that means I'm cool, and it's spelled 'phat.'"

When you were "bad" in my day, you had to stand in the corner. Nowadays bad means "cool" or "neat." Just when we think we've grasped the newest lingo, we find we are way behind the times again. According to the latest experts (my girls), it is now "tight" or "off the chain" when one refers to something being good or wonderful.

We are raised with phrases that we continue to use with our own children. I had gone with Courtney

◯ Perspectives from a "Smart" Christian

on a school trip, and she was kidding with some of the other kids and giving them a hard time. I told her, "Now, Courtney, don't be so ugly." The other kids gave me weird looks, but I didn't think anything about it. Later Courtney told me they said, "I can't believe your mom told you that you were ugly." Laughing, she said, "I told them you always say that to us when we misbehave and that you are not referring to our looks."

Words are powerful things. Answering someone in a sharp manner or tone can cause injured feelings or an incorrect interpretation of what a person really meant to say. I admonish my girls quite often to be careful what they say and how they say things to others. It is very easy to burst forth with a sharp retort in a moment of anger. It is much more difficult to fix the hurt of unkind words.

A few years ago, I had corrected Kalee about something she had done. She got very upset at me and began saying things she should not have said. Following her outburst, she promptly stomped off to her room. I decided to let her cool down a bit before confronting her. I was sitting on the couch in my bedroom when I noticed a piece of paper sliding under my bedroom door. I walked over and picked up the note she had written. It read, "Dear Mommy, I'm so sorry I got mad. What I said was on-call for." I began to chuckle as I read her apology. How many times had I said to her, "That is totally uncalled for"?

The Power of Words ↦

Yes, kids do pick up our words, and they are experts at mimicking adults. They learn how to live by watching us. We have to be careful that we present the right image to them. I, for one, am far from perfect. The girls can sense if I am worried, anxious, or upset, sometimes without my saying a word.

When we pastored in North Carolina, Courtney knew I was concerned about the finances of our church. While driving one day, we were listening to an exuberant choir song called "Stir Up the Gifts." She asked, "Mom, why don't you sing that for offering?" "What do you mean, Court?" I asked. She replied, "Well, they're saying, 'Shut up and give.' That would be a good song for offering." In her innocence, that seemed like a simple solution. However, I wonder how often we have had that very thought but we knew better than to put our thoughts into words.

Blaise Pascal said, "Cold words freeze people, and hot words scorch them, and bitter words make them bitter, and wrathful words make them wrathful. Kind words can produce their image on men's souls; and a beautiful image it is. They smooth, and quiet, and comfort the hearer."

Speak a kind word to those you meet. As the Word says, "Let the words of my mouth, and the meditation of my heart, be acceptable in thy sight, O LORD" (Psalm 19:14).

INTERVAL 16

Only God Can Change Lives, but We Can Help!

During our travels and pastoring through the years (makes me sound really old), I've noticed the frustration of people in winning others to God. Believe me, it is not always easy. However, I do not believe it is the will of God for us to become discouraged in our pursuit of souls.

When I was around thirteen years old, an evangelist came to our church in Texas. He was a great preacher and expounded the Word with a fierce voice and raised fist. Of course, I was taught by my godly parents that the ministry was always right and to heed what was preached. I remember one specific night the evangelist preached on winning souls. I listened intently because I wanted to do everything I could to serve God. However, he made one statement that stuck in my mind. He said, "If you are sitting here tonight and have not won a soul to God, you are going to hell."

◌ Perspectives from a "Smart" Christian

For several years, I carried that statement with me. I felt there was no hope for me. Here I was, the only UPC kid in my class, one of only a few UPC kids in my junior high who was trying to serve God. Pentecost was looked upon as a bizarre religion. These were the days before our type of worship had become popular in the religious world. People thought we were weird. However, I always had a hunger to win a soul. I tried every way I could to get someone to come to church with me, but they did not want anything to do with my religion. I finally convinced one of my friends who belonged to another denomination to spend a Friday night at my house and attend a youth rally. Well, you guessed it. The way we worshiped scared her to death! After that night, I was afraid of losing her friendship. When I got to school on Monday, she was talking to several of my other friends and was demonstrating what she called the "crazy" way we acted. I was humiliated. The rest of that week it seemed like the whole school was talking about my crazy church. I felt so defeated; I didn't think anyone would ever listen to me after my friend's rendition of our services.

The kids eventually seemed to forget about it, and thankfully the girl and I remained friends through the rest of high school. God blessed me by giving me lots of other friends as well. Even though a few visited church with me, no one seemed interested in receiving the Holy Ghost. I felt that I had failed God by not being the witness I should have been.

However, thank God I married someone who helped me see that it was not God's will for me to focus on that one evangelist's condemning statement. Sad to say, we found out later that the evangelist had fallen away from God and was no longer preaching. But the point my husband made was that the Bible says, "He that winneth souls is wise," and not "He that winneth not souls is going to hell." We have to be careful that we do not let our human concepts override the Word of God.

We live in a "now generation" of quick fixes, new, high-tech methods, and neat, easy-package plans. E-mail can be sent from outer space. Faxes and scanned images can be sent in a matter of moments. Everything is quick, quick, quick. But we must remember that a soul cannot always be won in such a quick manner.

Recently my parents received a phone call from a man who used to attend our home church. He told my parents that he had just heard a man preach about not realizing the influence you are having on those around you. He told about attending a small high school in Texas and noticing some girls who were consistent in serving God. They wore long dresses and had long hair. He always admired the "Smart girls" and knew they were Christians. When he decided to serve God, he found the religion that

◌ Perspectives from a "Smart" Christian

those "Smart girls" had. As I mentioned previously, my maiden name was Smart. I was so excited! Here I thought I had not affected anyone in my school, and now I find out years later that a United Pentecostal preacher had been influenced by my sister and me. Wow! What a neat feeling! And when I returned to my hometown for my class reunion, to my surprise, I found that some of the people from my class were members of our church in my hometown. So the life I lived in school was not totally in vain.

It is overwhelming to think that God could use me to help others. The influence of one godly life in a world of sin is a beautiful thing.

In finding the secret to soulwinning, we often think in terms of new approaches, special techniques, or mass-media advertising. But why not go to the master soulwinner of all time, the One we should imitate: "Be ye followers of me, even as I also am of Christ" (I Corinthians 11:1)? We should walk in His steps "because Christ also suffered for us, leaving us an example, that [we] should follow his steps" (I Peter 2:21). His influence upon people and the world was greater than anyone else who ever lived. He had a deep, abiding love and burden for lost souls. Nothing other than a determined purpose to reach the lost could have brought Jesus out of the ivory palaces to this lowly world of sin and sorrow. He felt the hurt of people and saw their need. "When he saw the multitudes, he was moved with compassion on them, because they fainted, and were scattered abroad, as sheep having no shepherd" (Matthew 9:36). His was not a planned program of soulwinning; it was His lifestyle.

Don't misunderstand me. We do need to give Bible studies and tell others about Christ. But just living for Jesus is an example all in itself. To influence others and lead them to Jesus, we must be like Jesus, walking like He walked and living in such a way that others watching our life will say, "I don't know what that person has, but I want some of it." Let the joy of the Lord control your life, and be a light in this world.

As my husband and I were eating at a restaurant, I overheard a conversation in the booth behind me. A little boy had asked his grandmother for some ice cream. She informed him that he had not eaten all of his supper, so he must be full. He kept trying to convince her that he needed the ice cream. She again told him that since he did not eat all of his food, he must be full. No ice cream was necessary if he was already full. "But, Grandma," he said, "you don't understand. I still have all of these empty spaces between those foods in my tummy. If I get some ice cream to eat, it will melt right into all of those empty places, and then I will be full."

Perhaps we could relate that to the world around us. There are people we meet daily who have empty spaces in their hearts. If we could just convince

◯ Perspectives from a "Smart" Christian

them of their need of Jesus, He could fill them with this precious Holy Ghost, and all of those empty spaces would be filled with His joy. Then they would really be full of God's presence.

Smile like never before. Talk like never before (I'm certain that will not be difficult for some of us, especially me) about Him. And live a life that is pleasing to God. Exemplify the joy God gave you.

The best tack in soulwinning is the impression you make on those with whom you come in contact.

—"Me"

Kindness has converted more sinners than zeal, eloquence, or learning.

—Frederick W. Faber

INTERVAL 17

Celebrating Friendships

Everyone needs friends. Lois Kaufman, an author, once said, "Plant a seed of friendship, reap a bouquet of happiness." Friends are important to us all. I think often of the Anne of Green Gables stories. One of Anne's greatest desires was to have a "bosom friend," someone with whom she could talk, share thoughts, cry, and rejoice.

Through the course of life, we will have many friends. At the toddler age, we socialize with children of our parents' friends. (We really don't have much choice at the age of two.) During elementary school, we develop a group of friends with whom we can bond.

In Mrs. Lemay's fifth-grade class, I found a "best friend." We were both part of another group of friends. A certain girl in our group chose the person to be mad at each week, for reasons that made no sense at all. However, by about mid-year, Jill and I

◠ Perspectives from a "Smart" Christian

wised up and parted from that group to become fast friends. Until the day we graduated, we remained the best of friends.

During college, another group of friends emerged. My parents moved to another city, and I came in contact with more friends. Following college, I made friends in the law firm in which I worked. And then I married my wonderful husband, my dearest friend.

This man of God and I evangelized for three years, and we met many wonderful friends. These friends were kind to us and taught us many things that would help us in our ministry.

The statement was once made that a true friend is among the most valuable of treasures. How true this is! I have some very close friends whom I treasure beyond measure.

One such friend has taught me etiquette, and I call her the Emily Post of Pentecost. When we are feeling down in the doldrums, she brings out her best teacups, and we drink tea as if we were high-society ladies. For some odd reason, this lifts our spirits. I always keep a fancy teacup on hand, just in case I need that escape from the doldrums.

Having tea together is something friends do. I read a story about a woman who believed a warm cup of tea would cure anything that ails a person. She wanted to serve tea to her parents, who had brought their friends from England to meet her. She put the

Celebrating Friendships ∽

kettle on and boiled and steeped the tea for the visitors. After she served the tea, she noticed that her guests would take a sip and quickly set their cups down. Thinking it was cold, she said, "Let me get you a fresh cup." Emphatically, they said that it wasn't necessary. "We've had plenty," they assured her.

After they had left, she began washing the cups and sensed that something was not quite right. Then it dawned on her. Her daughter had been suffering from a cold the night before, and she had poured a tablespoon of Vicks VapoRub in the kettle to use as a makeshift vaporizer to help her breathe. Afterward she had forgotten to soak the kettle. She had served the British visitors hot tea made with Vicks VapoRub! Frantically, she called her parents home and explained what had happened. They had a good laugh. The gentleman said that it was perfectly all right because when he came to her house, he was developing a cold. For some odd reason, after he drank her tea, he felt much better. Embarrassment gave way to humor because of the willingness to laugh and find something good in spite of what had happened. That's what friendship is all about.

Friends are there for you in the midst of your roughest times. When my husband and I received news of my pending brain surgery, I was devastated. Not long after we received the bad news, my husband tried to distract me by asking me to go with him on an unplanned trip to the airport to pick up

∽ Perspectives from a "Smart" Christian

some freight. Instead of the "freight," my Emily Post friend, Phyllis Jones, stepped off the plane! Tears of joy filled my eyes. Her visit gave me the reassurance I needed. What a wonderful weekend we enjoyed! It even snowed, which was an added blessing. Around a roaring fire, we talked, laughed, and reminisced. That weekend helped me to deal with my circumstances and to believe God had it all in control. My mourning turned to laughing, all because of my friend!

I have definitely reaped a bouquet of happiness through all of our awesome friends. Friends have continued to enter our life, until the abundance is so great that I feel blessed beyond measure to have so many friends in God's kingdom.

The Joy of Friendship

Bring a friend with you to shop, and your joy increases. "Friends are a great distraction from our woes, and having someone to laugh at or admire what you find is twice as much fun as shopping alone."

When you share something fun with a friend, perhaps a decadent sweet treat, your body produces lots of extra oxytocin, an anti-stress hormone. You get double the pleasure from the "friend experience."

—Contributed by Deborah Cooper, Ph.D.

Spending a few minutes venting to a friend will put you in a happier mood. Research shows holding worries in makes them fester, while voicing them validates your feelings and lets you move on.

—Robin Kowalski, Ph.D., Author of
*Complaining, Teasing and Other
Annoying Behaviors*

INTERVAL 18

Tough Times

You may be in the midst of a struggle, and no solution seems forthcoming. Some well-meaning individual (this type is in abundance) shares some encouraging words with you: "Tough times make tough people." "Okay," you may say, wondering how this helps. Though the statement may be true, it does not tend to encourage me. Instead, it sounds like something a drill sergeant might scream at recruits.

We are in this world, and there are going to be times when struggle becomes a part of our lives. How we handle that struggle is very important. I have often heard my husband say, "It's not what happens in life; it's how you take what happens." It all comes down to how we deal with life.

Everyone has her own way of coping with struggle, whether it is something she dreads or something she may fear. When Kara was about two and one-half

∞ Perspectives from a "Smart" Christian

years old, she was afraid of shadows. My parents had a long hallway that led to their bedrooms, and they kept a nightlight burning in the hallway. While toddling down the hallway one day, Kara saw a black thing following her. She ran crying to us that something black was following her. My mother and I both tried to explain to her the shadow phenomenon, but her little mind could not seem to comprehend it. She could not understand why her little body made a black thing on the wall. It was scary! Finally, I told her that her shadow was friendly and that it would not hurt her. Therefore, she needed to be friendly to her shadow. When she walked down that long hall, if she saw her shadow, she could wave at it and it would wave back. I am not a child psychologist nor do I hold a counseling degree, but this definitely worked for us. It was so cute to see our little sweetheart start down that hallway and immediately begin waving and calling, "Hi, Shadow. Hi, Shadow." Her reaction when she saw the shadow waving back was awesome. And it certainly made me feel like one smart mama.

How wonderful it would be if every situation were as easy to solve as our shadow situation! I know that is not always the case, but if we take a little time to try to find a solution to our problem through the Word of God and prayer, it would make things so much easier. I usually try to take care of everything myself and often find myself praying,

Tough Times

"God, help me to realize I cannot do this on my own. I need Your help."

A dear friend of our family, Linda Elms, shared a cute story with me about her granddaughter. One night the little girl did not want to stay in her room and go to sleep because she was scared. Her mother patiently explained to her that Jesus was in her room, that He would always be with her, and she could feel His presence. Then the mother prayed a simple prayer asking for God's blessing and protection and got up to leave the room. Just as she opened the door to walk out, the little girl cried out, "But I can't feel God. I need my daddy."

It may take more than just a simple prayer to give us reassurance. Sometimes we have to get on our knees and earnestly seek the Lord for the answer we need. He will always have the answer. It may not be the answer we want, but it will be the answer that is best for us. Psalm 1:6 says, "The LORD knoweth the way of the righteous." What a comfort to know that the Lord knows exactly where we are: under the shadow of a trial or on the sunny mountaintop of a victory. He is with us always!

I received an e-mail entitled "Christian One-Liners." I enjoyed reading it, especially since it began with my last name. One of the quotes read, "God promises a safe landing, not a calm passage."

Yes, we may question what happens in our lives. We may not understand the trouble that threatens to

Perspectives from a "Smart" Christian

swamp our boat, but if we can train ourselves to see the bright side and look for good in a bad situation, we will eventually reach the safe harbor.

The story is told of a young woman who became extremely ill. Upon going to the doctor, she found that she had a terminal illness and had only a few months to live. She contacted her pastor and asked him to meet with her about the funeral arrangements. Thinking that he would find the young lady in despair, he came prepared to minister to her. Instead, the pastor found her serene and calm as they discussed her funeral arrangements. Just as the pastor was preparing to leave, she excitedly said, "Oh, there is one more thing I would like to request."

"And what might that be?" he asked.

The young lady answered, "I wish to be buried with a fork in my right hand." The pastor looked at the young lady in disbelief. "But why?" he asked.

The young lady explained, "My grandmother once told me that when she attended social events, they often would say, 'Keep your fork,' when clearing the table. My grandmother said it was her favorite part of the meal because she knew that something better and sweeter was coming—like velvety chocolate cake or deep-dish apple pie. So I want people to see me in the casket with a fork in my hand. When they ask you what the fork is for, I want you to tell them this story so they will know that for me the best is yet to come."

Tough Times ~

I am not certain I could have the same type of outlook as this young lady, but I pray that I can look for the good in my times of struggle. I want to be able to know that no matter what happens, God has my life in His hands.

John Adams, one of the founding fathers of our wonderful country, suffered much for his participation in establishing a new government for a new country. He was a learned man who spent a great deal of time in thought trying to find the best solution for a country torn by war. I was struck by one of the statements he made in his writings: "People and nations are forged in the fires of adversity." Thus we become who we are by "going through the fires" of life.

Joy Haney, the first lady of the United Pentecostal Church International, recently published a book entitled, *Gold Tried In the Fire*. In the book she recounts the process used in the old days for purifying gold. The goldsmith would submit the ore to extreme heat that ultimately separated the precious gold from worthless alloy. When the fire brought the gold to the temperature where impurity could no longer stay, the goldsmith could see his reflection in the molten metal. At that point, he knew the gold was purified and had reached a final stage of malleability and value. So is the process of life. God uses the heat and pressure of uncomfortable, stressful, or painful life experiences to remove the impurities from our lives.

◠ Perspectives from a "Smart" Christian

Although we would like to avoid the tough times, they are for our good. If we handle them correctly, we can come out of the fire much better people and thanking God for bringing us to another level in Him.

Optimism is akin to faith. Pessimism is akin to doubt. To which are you akin?
— *Quotable Quotes*: Compiled by LLOYD CORY

God wants us to be victors, not victims; to grow, not grovel; to soar, not sink; to overcome, not to be overwhelmed.

—WILLIAM A. WARD

INTERVAL 19

And How Do You Like Your Job?

Working is a fact of life. Thanks to Adam and Eve, our garden paradise was destroyed when they chose to do something God specifically commanded them not to do. He was "their boss," yet they did not want to submit to His request. Thus we have to toil daily.

After high school, I decided to attend college and had big plans to get a fabulous job. However, God switched my plan in midstream. Although I had no intention of being a minister's wife, I am one. And what an interesting and challenging position it has been!

Prior to my minister's wife position, I graduated from college and God blessed me with a great job at a law firm in Amarillo, Texas. I made friends with a few of the other ladies there and often ate lunch with them. One day a friend and I went to lunch with one of our other coworkers, who worked in the finance

Perspectives from a "Smart" Christian

department of the law firm. All during lunch, she talked about who was getting paid the most, who did not deserve it, or who seemed to get by with things. She spent our whole lunch hour—a time that was supposed to be relaxing—griping about the unfairness of our firm. My friend and I had gone to lunch thankful for our positions, but we came back with a negative attitude. We wondered if our firm was that great after all. This one lady had influenced us to doubt the blessing we thought we had. Thankfully, we returned to thinking about the good things our firm had to offer and how generous it was to us with good benefits and bonuses. We were able to change the attitude the lady had infiltrated into our minds. Needless to say, we avoided going to lunch with her again.

After my husband and I married, I left my job and started evangelizing with him. I thought at the time that I would probably not work a secular job any more, but that would not be the case. I realize now that God allowed me to attend college and obtain a degree in order to help benefit His kingdom. When my husband and I were in a home missions work, He blessed me with another good job so that my husband could focus on building a church.

God has blessed me with some great places to work. However, no place is perfect. How you perceive your job will depend on your attitude. I have seen some unhappy people in the workforce, and in

And How Do You Like Your Job?

observing their habits, I can see why they are unhappy. I have found one thing to be true. The majority of people want to be in control or have the most power. Thus, when they cannot seem to attain their goal, they become cantankerous. If they would choose to get along with others instead of causing conflict and difficulty in every situation, the workplace would be more harmonious.

The story is told of a mother preparing pancakes for her sons, Kevin, five, and Ryan, three. The boys began to argue over who would be the first one served. Their mother saw the chance to teach the boys a lesson. She said, "If Jesus were sitting here, He would say, 'Let my brother have the first pancake. I can wait.'" Kevin turned to his younger brother and said, "Ryan, you be Jesus!"

Although humorous, this story is true to life. Desiring to be the top one seems to be the nature of the human race. Got to be first, got to be number one. Sad to say, at times I have found myself resenting the role of a servant. It is not an easy job. In Ephesians 6:5, Paul gave instructions to those in service: "Servants, be obedient to them that are your masters according to the flesh, with fear and trembling, in singleness of your heart, as unto Christ."

You may have "arrived" as the one in charge. However, most people are accountable to someone, whether it is a supervisor or a boss. We need to treat our boss or supervisor with respect as the Word of

꩜ Perspectives from a "Smart" Christian

God instructs us. We should not backbite those in leadership or try to undercut them in our efforts to look good. Backbiting or undercutting will almost certainly guarantee that the boss will not look on you as someone with potential leadership abilities. Instead, it could cause you to remain at entry level in the workforce.

As born-again children of God, we should all the more exemplify proper work ethics. So before shooting an e-mail that lets someone know just who they're dealing with, take a moment to think about your actions. Would Jesus send such an e-mail, the One who knelt before His "laborers" and washed their feet, the One who shed His life's blood that we might live? He became a servant as an example of how we must live. I Corinthians 9:19 says, "For though I be free from all men, yet have I made myself servant unto all, that I might gain the more."

While living in North Carolina, I decided to seek a part-time position for my own peace of mind. Being the pastor's wife was at times stressful and demanding, so I thought getting away for a while would be the perfect solution. I found a promising ad in the newspaper and sent my résumé to a law office. That very afternoon, I received a call from a nice attorney named Paul Shepard. He asked that I come in for an interview, which ended up with my being hired that day. Paul was a very pleasant and accommodating person. While working for him, I saw how diligently

And How Do You Like Your Job?

he tried to help disabled clients and to do the best he could in every case he accepted. He was more than an attorney. He really cared about people.

Paul belonged to another denomination, but we did have the opportunity to discuss God on numerous occasions. I invited him to be in service with us on Friend's Day, and he was kind enough to come and support our efforts. The day following his visit, I found a note on my desk. I cannot remember the note verbatim, but it read something like this: "Karla, Thank you for inviting me to your church. I enjoyed everything so much—the music and Mark's sermon. But I guess the thing I enjoyed the most was the joy I felt there. I hope to visit again soon. Sincerely, Paul."

We should try our best to exude the joy of the Lord in our workplace. It may not be the most perfect environment, but we need to thank God for providing a place for us and ask that He help us to be content. How you act in the office will affect whether people will want to become acquainted with your church, which is a major factor in God's plan.

Also, since we spend more of our waking hours on the job than at home, we should make every effort to enjoy our job. We should try our best to work well with others and be accommodating, instead of creating difficulties for our coworkers. Not only will we benefit ourselves; we will also benefit those we are around by showing them what true Christianity is.

Perspectives from a "Smart" Christian

In a previous chapter, I mentioned a research conclusion from Emory University which I believe bears reiterating here. Cooperating with another person activates the pleasure centers of the brain. During tests, those who chose to work together responded much better to games and activities. Life always works better when we work together.

So since the question "And how do you like your job?" usually comes up while making polite conversation, have a positive answer ready. Here is another chance to find the good in an important part of your life.

Nothing is harder work than not having a job.
—Franklin P. Jones

INTERVAL 20

How Do You Affect Your Atmosphere?

A few months ago, while I reviewed some notes for a ladies' meeting during which I was scheduled to speak, Courtney, my middle daughter, was sitting with me trying to help me locate tidbits on a certain subject. All of a sudden, she broke into laughter. Of course, if anyone is laughing, I certainly want to know why so that I can laugh too. She was reading a feature article in the Reader's Digest entitled, "Headlines That Hurt." She said, "Mom, listen to these. 'Iraqi Head Seeks Arms.' 'Teacher Strikes Idle Kids.' 'Police Begin Campaign to Run Down Jaywalkers.'" We spent a few minutes laughing at the ridiculous headlines.

What better way to have joy in our lives than by making laughter a part of them? Proverbs 15:13 says, "A merry heart maketh a cheerful countenance: but by sorrow of the heart the spirit is broken." Likewise, Proverbs 17:22 says, "A merry heart doeth good like a medicine." And one of my favorites is Proverbs 15:15: "He that is of a merry heart hath a continual feast."

Erma Bombeck, a well-known author who wrote many humorous articles and books, said a child once asked the question, "Does God laugh?" She said, "I don't know if He does or not, but He sure fixed me where I could." A blurb in *USA Today* reported that children laugh an average of four hundred times a day, whereas an adult chuckles only about fifteen times.

So why do children laugh so much? Perhaps it's because they have not yet learned to doubt everything they hear and see. They laugh with glee over simple things. Life is one exciting event after another. As adults, we get so wrapped up in our own affairs that we forget that God is God and we're not.

One day a grandma was baby-sitting her grandson. The little boy said, "Grandma, do you know how you and God are alike?" Feeling quite good about the child comparing her to God and mentally polishing her halo, she asked, "No, how are we alike?" "You're both old," he answered.

Yes, as we age (which I know I don't like to think about), our joy may wane. One grandmother was telling her little granddaughter what her own childhood was like: "We used to skate outside on a pond. I had a tire swing that hung from a tree in our front yard. We would swing on it and laugh and yell as we soared through the air." The little girl with wide eyes was taking all this information in. At last she said, "I sure wish I had gotten to know you sooner."

One benefit of laughter is that it is contagious. One day while grocery shopping with two-year-old Courtney, I experienced how contagious it can be. She got the giggles, and she had an infectious giggle. I began noticing the people's reactions to her belly laughs. Frowns turned to smiles. Some people even started laughing with her. Right there in the produce department, we had a laughter revival. People began smiling at each other and talking about the laughing little girl. The whole atmosphere changed because of a joyful little girl.

No matter how bad things are in life, there is always something good for which we can thank God. The choice is ours. We can focus on our problems, or we can focus on the goodness of God. If we focus on our problems, we are going into the self-centeredness mode: my problems, my issues, my pain. Believe me, I have been there a few times. But one of the easiest ways to get rid of pain is to get your focus off yourself and onto God and others. We can share the joy that God has put into our lives with others around us. I would love to be able to influence others and help change their atmospheres just like Courtney did in the grocery store.

◌ Perspectives from a "Smart" Christian

◌ ◌ ◌ ◌ ◌ ◌

Some cause happiness wherever they go. Some whenever they go.

—S<small>POTLIGHT</small>

INTERVAL 21

Ending on a Happy Note

The Scriptures give us many examples pertaining to joy. Nehemiah 8:10 tells us the joy of the Lord is our strength. I Chronicles 16:27 tells us that strength and joy are in God's dwelling place. John 16:24 tells us to ask and receive so that our joy may be full. No matter what definition of joy we use—abundance, happiness, or fulfillment—our relationship with God is integral to true joy.

What helps bring joy to our lives? I believe that the laughter mechanism God placed in us plays a big part. Laughter is the best medicine. In the last few months, since I have been studying this wonderful mechanism, I have noticed numerous reports discussing the benefits of laughter. One such article appeared in the *Reader's Digest*, called "Laugh and Live Longer."

According to the author, this inherent phenomenon of laughter is a preset program that involves the entire body. Scientists felt that this happiness issue deserved

⚭ Perspectives from a "Smart" Christian

some major research to find out the full benefits of a good laugh. They actually put people into MRI machines and made them laugh. (I have e-mailed the digest to see where I might apply for this type of job. However, I don't think they would have to make me laugh because I already have overactive laughter. Just ask my family and friends.) Anyway, during this intricate research, it was proved for the first time that laughter stimulates the parts of the brain that use the "feel-good" chemical messenger, dopamine. Dopamine (sounds somewhat like "dope am I") systems that get out of whack can lead to addiction. One Emory University neurologist, Gregory Burns, concluded, "Laughter is pleasurable, perhaps even addictive to the brain." Perhaps that is why, once my three girls start laughing, it is difficult for them to cease.

No matter what noise you make when you laugh—a snicker, a snort, a giggle, or a blast—laughter follows a precise recipe. It relaxes the face, the tear ducts activate, and glands create saliva with higher levels of disease-fighting agents called immunoglobins. (That word itself causes me to laugh.) It activates our vocal cord system, causes our lungs to exchange much more air than normal, and enriches our blood with oxygen. It even helps our heart. When we laugh, we get a shot of good chemicals, like nitric oxide, which reduces clotting and inflammation.

Whew! I feel like an anatomy teacher. I know you are impressed by my knowledge. Ironically, even though scientists have spent lots of money and time to find the benefits of laughter, the Lord already told us to be happy. The Bible refers to the joy of the Lord or gladness of heart over eight hundred times. And I know how much better I feel when I laugh. It is a given.

If perhaps I haven't convinced some of you yet as to the benefits of laughter, let me cover one last reason. This is my favorite: we can laugh ourselves skinny. The more we laugh, the more calories we burn.

After a session of monitoring a group of people equipped with calorie-counting device, Vanderbilt University researchers found that laughing increased the heart rate by 10 to 20 percent and burned about 1.3 calories per minute. Thus laughter is exercise. Lee Beck, a prominent scientist, said, "Laughter is really jogging for your insides." We can forget those ab machines! We can laugh our way to health and beauty.

Dr. William Fry of Stanford University said that laughing heartily a hundred times a day has the same beneficial effect as ten minutes on the rowing machine. So, let's review. Laughter increases heart rate and circulation, stimulates the immune system, and improves the muscle tone of the abdomen. Laughter also jogs for us and burns calories. Isn't that fantastic? We have found the secret to shedding those pounds.

To summarize all of this jargon, researchers and scientists have found that laughter is of great benefit

○○ Perspectives from a "Smart" Christian

to our health and peace of mind and is a pleasurable phenomenon. Well, God's Word already told us that. His Word continually tells us to be joyful.

A few years ago, I went through a pretty traumatic experience. I developed an aneurysm and the medical team found I had some additional problems with my brain. At least they found out I had a brain! We have what they call "tonsils" in the brain, and my particular tonsils had fallen into the spinal cord area, leaving a space in my brain. (I was relieved to find out that I really did have a reason for being spacey. Now, I don't know what my excuse is.)

To make a long story short, the mercy of God spared my life. We were told that I would not recover the movement in my left side and that I would most likely have to go through rehab to be able to walk properly. But that was not the final outcome. Following nine hours of surgery, to the glory of God, I could again feel my left side and knew everything was going to be fine. Oh, I still have side effects—headaches and weird sensations of imbalance—but I am here to glorify God and thank Him for bringing me this far. And yes, laughter does help me get through the tough times that come every now and then. I thank God for the joy and the reassurance He has given to me in spite of the circumstances.

I desire more than anything to change my world with the joy God has given me. Oh, I know that we face difficult problems every day, but God has given

Ending on a Happy Note ↔

us the mechanism of laughter. He put it there for a reason; it helps us get through the difficult times.

Isaiah 51:11 gives us the promise that everlasting joy shall be ours: "Therefore the redeemed of the LORD shall return, and come with singing unto Zion; and everlasting joy shall be upon their head."

So, I would like to end my *bookella* on a happy note. I hope some thoughts or words have helped you to laugh or chuckle. I trust that you have found a renewal of joy in life. I know that life is not always easy. It is perhaps harder for some than for others. But there is a way to find joy in the journey of life. You can experience joy in the moment, regardless of the circumstances. You have access to the wonderful gift of the Holy Ghost, and that gift alone gives you the capacity to live a joyful life. You can indeed choose to be joyful.

Radiate the joy of the Lord, and give out joy to those in your circle of influence. You don't have to base happiness on what happens. You can make the choice to rejoice. You can look for the good even in times of crisis. Take time to smile at someone in the grocery store. Take time to speak to someone while you're at the mall. Perhaps that smile or word of kindness can give a bereft person hope that there really is someone who cares. You care because Jesus Christ cared enough to die for you. Share with others the joy He so willingly gave, and experience that fullness of joy every day of your life.